GOING HOME

Going Home

Poems
by
DONNY BARILLA

Adelaide Books
New York / Lisbon
2019

GOING HOME
Poems
By Donny Barilla

Copyright © by Donny Barilla
Cover design © 2019 Adelaide Books

Published by Adelaide Books, New York / Lisbon
adelaidebooks.org

Editor-in-Chief
Stevan V. Nikolic

All rights reserved. No part of this book may be reproduced in any manner whatsoever without written permission from the author except in the case of brief quotations embodied in critical articles and reviews.

For any information, please address Adelaide Books
at info@adelaidebooks.org
or write to:
Adelaide Books
244 Fifth Ave. Suite D27
New York, NY, 10001

ISBN-10: 1-950437-80-9
ISBN-13: 978-1-950437-80-1

Printed in the United States of America

Dedicated to Nash and Darla
Thank you for the memories and the beautiful friendship

Contents

Gluttony *17*

Stillness *18*

Watching for Summer *19*

As the Wind Touched *20*

Eaves and the Living Rain *21*

Stitch of Evening *22*

Storm by Stream and Forest *23*

After a Travel to the East *24*

Mouth of the Dragon *25*

Sleeping on the Earth/Wet Beds of Soil *26*

The Ache of Brotherhood *27*

The Galaxy *28*

Dust *29*

Recollection *30*

Summer Storm *31*

Peering upon the Grassy Pasture *32*

By Doorstep *33*

Empty Garments *34*

Ivory *35*

Love Poem *36*

Fields of Wheat *37*

Autumn Flowers *38*

Lost *39*

March, 2018 *40*

Gardener *41*

A Distance from Summer *42*

Mumbling Voices *43*

Baking in Breads *44*

Elm Leaf *45*

Follow *46*

Grove *47*

Marinade *48*

Memorial Day, 2017 *49*

Last Evening in the Forest *50*

Resting *51*

Listening to Seagulls *52*

Flesh and Fog *53*

Slumber *54*

Patiently Awaiting *55*

Drought *56*

Spring Visitation *57*

Stillness of the Water *58*

Fig *59*

By Pond *60*

Lakes Edge *61*

Gestures *62*

End of Day *63*

Warmth of the Sun *64*

Resurrection *65*

Thinking of You after a Rainstorm *66*

Soft Rain *67*

Settling Dust *68*

Crackling Night *69*

Coveted Clays *70*

Tumble and Dance *71*

Dreamed *72*

Waiting a Year *73*

Morning Dream *74*

From Spring to Spring *75*

Picnic *76*

After Nightfall into Deep of Morning *77*

Waiting in the Evergreen *78*

Breath *79*

Country Walking *80*

Searching *81*

Fondling Quartz **82**

Resting by the Stream **83**

Roaming with Nightfall **84**

Asleep by the Ocean's Cove **85**

Into my Lungs **86**

A Place of Light and Rest **87**

Vanish **88**

Night I Covet **89**

Pebble **90**

Morning Time **91**

Age **92**

Lime Green **93**

Toward Mountains Peak **94**

Seeds **95**

Groaning Lilacs **96**

Nightfall **97**

Upon these Hills **98**

Eclipse **99**

After a Rest in Avalon **100**

Cloudy Morning **101**

Shattered Woods **102**

Traveling East **103**

Distant Fires **104**

Spending Time Alone by the River **105**

GOING HOME

Bedtime Stories   *106*
Teardrops   *107*
Gripped in the Fog   *108*
Chestnuts and Apricots   *109*
Fire Pit   *110*
Alone   *111*
Curving Bones   *112*
Valley Invites   *113*
Winter Defeat   *114*
Going Home   *115*
By the Ocean   *116*
Childhood Dreaming   *117*
Walk along the Beach   *118*
Birds at Play   *119*
Remembrance During a Snowy Night   *120*
Dreamt by Moonlight   *121*
Tangerine Sky   *122*
Voice of the Woods   *123*
Near   *124*
Soothing Ferns   *125*
River Curves through Mist   *126*
Waiting on the Crow   *127*
When the Mist Settles   *128*
As Light Beckons   *129*

Rising Sun *130*

Vanish *131*

From Every Stitch *132*

Pasture *133*

Looking upon Twilight *134*

Observing the Shadow *135*

From Woods Alone *136*

Gathering in the Edge of the Woods *137*

Fallen Youth *138*

From Home to the Unburdening Bay *139*

Seasons by the Bay *140*

As the Sky Spreads *141*

Guidance *142*

Parting *143*

Morning Alone *144*

The Willow Tree *145*

Spreading Lips by Moonlight *146*

Orchid *147*

Throwing Rocks *148*

Oak *149*

Soft Thoughts *150*

Forested Hills *151*

Loosening Blouse *152*

Osprey *153*

The Pear Tree   *154*

Soils and Blackbirds   *155*

Standing by the Fence   *156*

Diamond   *157*

Star Gazing   *158*

Shuffled Leaves   *159*

Camp   *160*

Idle Passages   *161*

Fog's Arrival   *162*

Clarity Waits   *163*

Elder Trees   *164*

Watching Crows   *165*

Fields Tucked between Mountains   *166*

Thin Lips   *167*

Afternoon Moisture   *168*

Passage   *169*

Robe   *170*

Soft   *171*

As the Trees Echo   *172*

Veils   *173*

Acorn   *174*

Mountains and Forests   *175*

Cove   *176*

Eastern Trail   *177*

About the Author   *179*

I sink to the flesh of the red skinned apple...

Songs from a bard, resound through the winds tugging through a restless forest.

Approaching, coming closer, I hear the perfection of his voice.

I feel the winds splash through the loose, fine fibers of my hair.

Gluttony

The pebbled road took me, my feet along a journey,
raspy in a jaunt in the sacred wood.

The evergreen stood along the mountains edge
and wisped with the threading winds.
Each pine cone, chipped in the fallen beds, gathered
amongst each other and layered as rugged gatherings.

A year later, I stood in the orchard and soothed to
the scents of peaches which gloated upon the softest earth.

I sank my teeth to the tender flesh
while juices seeped along the rim of my mouth
and I settled fangs to the pulps- warm fuzz.

A year later, I groomed in the endless woods.
So lost, I picked my feet into the clever roots
which uttered a breath of each fresh soil.

Stillness

She lay as a cocoon, permeating through
each wool fiber and thread.
Specks of hovering dust danced along her body
roaming as she coiled naked from opened arms to full breasts.

Pressing upon the fossil of her bed,
I trembled to the sounds of the blackbird
jousting about her garden. From near
to distant flock and hue
The birds filled the air as a choir of soothing hymns.

Peering out the fogged, sweaty window,
I flickered my eyes to the soaking silver moon.

With a dull glow, the lone oak in the gardens grotto
threw a bold and nude shadow across each print of the yard.

Watching for Summer

Cool air shrouded. I stood still, chilled by the gush of river,
and nearby pond which opened as the bow of a oak tree,
inviting with trembling water, filled with kelp and soot.

Leafy parchment flickered across the ground.
I knelt, placed one in my opened palm,
then, in a smooth gust of wind, I watched as
each rippling wave of each passing water

Nabbed the leaf and swallowed it to the basin of the channel
so close to the bank.

Later, when the seasons flashed to heavy Summer,
I drank the water born so aligned with the earth.

Into the damp and rich cloak of nightfall,
I slid my fingers in a scrape along the soil
and heard the stones rattle beneath
water and soot.

As the Wind Touched

I spoke of the trembling wind when all soothed still.
Dance through the bed of clovers, I begged for the sky
which tore each thread of this bequeathing breath.

There lurked a softness as I tugged fingers and thumbs;
the lusts of the scouring grass begged for more.

~

She asked me to scatter kisses across her pale chest,
I softly smiled
and looked away.

I could feel the wind through my face
and hazelnut colored hair.

Eaves and the Living Rain

Soft, the sapling wiggled, fiddled through the wind,
patterned across the chrome blue sky.

Holding the smallness of her hand,
I cast a smile upon her as giggles came forth.

Roaming through the stiff emerald blades
tiny pebbles rolled from palm to pocket.

~

I filled my lungs with aroma and glimmering fragrance.

The sweet spices swept from the winds,
tangled upon my tongue.

~

I sat her upon my leg and watched as her fingers
tumbled each rolling pebble.

Warm winds slipped both approaching rain and the dance
of smashing lightning. We walked to the eaves of the house;
softly, she hugged my leg.

Stitch of Evening

As a gash, the tender pink hush of evening
opened across the horizon and bled the softest
yellow fade of the sun.

From the cavern of my throat,
I pronounced the bedded threads called, "night."

With patterns soothing in navy and quiet indigo,
each loose leaf rolled slowly across the lawns and patios.

Quite close, I wept beneath the evergreen trees
which gathered sparsely, rolling each needle and cone.
I thought of her and trembled with the fever of her
once opened blouse, the calm of the stitch
and bend of the hem, cultured me in roaming rhythms.

Storm by Stream and Forest

The throaty slaps of the sweet sauntering stream,
dripped along as ointments to the bald face
of the rocks and scattered pebbles lining the shore.

I lifted my face and wedged my neck to the thick
lumbering tree branch soothing behind me
and said, "I place my thumbs and fingers to my
temples and sulk them to my sweat soaked hair.
Thrive through me as the pulsing stream and the dance
of the approaching storm. Sap across the basin
of my mouth and swab me in your loving spirit."

With the breath of each spindling wind and gust,
I turned and faced the gnarled forest
which groomed across me in leafy pastures.

After a Travel to the East

I face east to the risen hill,
Wet blades dampen my boots.

I reach to summit where the sun glances,
Warms the roaming grass.

Softly, I watch the dreaming sycamore
Tremble after each splash of wind.

Looking back, I see the forest as it threads
And weaves through the valley.

Longingly, I descend.

Travelling to the supple shroud of shattered leaves
Dancing upon the shattered woodland floor,

I return, only to taste the creeks water
Which sulk across the wedge of my feet and legs.

I stand enamored as the shuffling leaves
Seduce every drop of water and wind.

Mouth of the Dragon

The sky hummed in paintings of pink, purple, satin blue.
I felt the soft winds sulk along my lips and angles
of my face as I turned to face the rise of the east.

By the middle of day, the winds excited to the open
mouth of a dragon, wailing upon the sacred sky.

I fell to the resins of the earth and dipped my toes
to the emeralds of the perfect clover.

There sulked passions swimming about the sky.
I stepped to the gnarled root and sat so quiet,
watching the smashing rains dampen, murmuring muds.

Sleeping on the Earth/Wet Beds of Soil

The haze, cream colored moon
roped about the oak tree
as nightfall blushed and tossed
a masked drape of fog
which hummed as a serving dish
rattling the counter tops.

I placed a dozen acorns in the depth, so deep
in my pockets.

By morning, the clouds lifted. They vanished
into the pouches of the earth by where
I slept.

Walking home, harmless and hungry,
baskets of rain fell from the sky,
sulking and begging.

The Ache of Brotherhood

I stood against the endless wall of brick
aching feet and mourning heels,
gently I leaned my sore head back
and with a quiet quiver I watched the coin
slip from the pouch and roll for a few seconds among
the tallest grass and gnarled weed.

Here, I hold no dominion.
I sweat the silence which slaps around my head.

~

That time, a year later
I sank into the pebbly soil and slept
gingerly, I felt the wind caress my lathering mud.

~

There slipped a press against my lip
and I spoke of you, brotherhood,
stooping and stepping upon my chest.

How slowly I yearn for you.

The Galaxy

A quiet steam rose silently above the lake.
From an endless distance, I could feel the smoothest
trickle of her breath
as the night's moon opened from clouds passing,
riddling me in softness.

With my palm,
I touched the bareness of my mouth
and swayed to a damp fever.

After looking to the cottony spreading sky,
I sliced my fingers through the mist coated air
returning to the satin finish of the water,
I slouched and slumbered in twitch and dew drops
which possessed galaxies on my tongue.

I sink my fingers where the marrow bleeds.

Dust

By the old brick home, I thought of you.
With the cracked adjacent windows, your
breath softened the air surrounding me.

Warmth of the fireplace,
licked me in tongues from flame to a tremoring pale light.
I recall the slipping fingers which once roamed
the cheeks of my face. Lips which rose my skin
to thick pockets of swaggering heat.

Passages of days end, I sat quietly
on the ancient wooden boards, here on this patio.

I looked upon the overgrowth of the riddled, dead
garden. Smelling the onion grass, you spoke to me
of decay when the moon shrouds and the earth
in all it's marrow, wraps in the cottons a frigid cocoon.

Walking through the thicket spread, the yellow grasses
of the grotto where nothing grows in a decisive manner.

You drape across me and I breath your dusty
touch delving through to my decanter of lungs.

I turn swiftly and jaunt to the endless
roads from which I came.

Recollection

Walking the endless rows of barley, I
dredged through with grains
flouting both pollens and seed, pampering the already thick
skin, stretched in a sun doused leather grip.

I smiled as the crows fed upon the richness of this soil.
She grew damp as the rain began, splattering muds.

The gloat of the clouds dripped across the fading sun
and I heard her whisper through each verb of pouring
drizzle. Gently, I felt the fingers of you, now

bones which quiver to me. I walk endlessly and return to you
with the heaviness of my boots.

Summer Storm

Gales rattled the treetops. Birch woods shred shavings
as each branch hooked and broke to the woodland floor.

Lightning fell as jaws to the soaking earth.
In a moment, we felt the wet pastes of our
clothing sulked to our backs and arms.

Standing where you once lay, spread open
as lavender and sweet scents of scattered mint,

I wade through the forests mud;
I heard you call my name which pressed

forth with the birch wood, clapping against thunder,
roaming through the breath of crackling wind.

I search for the scent of you as I wade thigh deep
in the thicket of Summer heat, now cooling
as rains chilled by the spreading glimpse of nightfall.

Peering upon the Grassy Pasture

Fangs of slippery ice trellised across the eaves.
I listened to the rain as puddles stung the heavy slabs
of stone and mortar.

~

I watched her grow to the thick snowy pasture
which coddled her name in each press
of growling wind.

By Spring, her scent loafed through the breeze.
Her mouth yearned as the quiet buds
of each branch, boasting the greens of each tree.

~

When the madness of the gales came, I
wrestled to the absence of her touch.

Looking to the farthest distance of sloping fields,
I recalled the soils where we last kissed.

By Doorstep

When we roamed each surface:
delving creek, grass blown meadow,
forests damp with majesty, you would
place the chill of your hand along my sweat dipped neck
and speak of each chip of the bone
which wrestled both mulch and hidden clays.

I smile and return you to the earth.
So alive with chewing rains, preserving
your thick pasture of hair and quiet smile-
forever crimped this gown, the silent soil.
Textures of your nakedness fill my lungs and vacant mouth.

Rains of this heavy March day penetrate.
I dampen to the white drops, scattered across the field.

I reach the hearth of this feeble home.
Removing my boots, I welcome you to this doorstep
where I pause and rest quick into night.

Empty Garments

I sweeten my mouth to the berries of your flesh.
You speak to me in tongues, a language as ancient
as the moon and burning as the sun.

Finding corridors,
my sleeves, filled with tender arms,
crown the pastes of your neck and temples.

Into the madness of this clever hour, I spread
across you as the garments sulking across the wooden floor.

~

I awaken in the trembling hour of dawn.
You leave the softest trace of silver dust
glinting upon your pillow.

I can smell your breath long into the morning.

Ivory

The row boat slips across the chill of the lake.
Crisp as the stiffest sheets, the water
sleeps in hushing slumber
as I pause by the swollen cove -moss and mud
slithered by the edge of the shoreline.

You sit still and pensive.
I stir to the fragrance of your milky breasts.
Into the glancing press of morning
I hear you breath and witness the rising clouds.

Thin, the cottons unfold.
Mist settles, tapping the water's film
which begins to recede upon the length of day.

I lean across an endless pocket of space.
Her gentle kiss soothes tender and the clouds lift
threading spools of rippled waves open as a dance
where her climate hangs in the palest
creams of an ivory sunset.

Love Poem

The reaching curve of your sloping back
quivers beneath my calm fingers.

Out my door, the snow flecks upon the early grass.
Now March and the blossoms and buds
wash in the sting of a drifting Winter.

~

The slice of the fleshed apple groom
baskets which boast of pulps and milks.

I carry scents, musk, to the crest of your appetite.
I feel the fangs of your fingers pull stiffly
upon the groin of the grassy earth.

~

Now nearing April and I delve in the richness
of Spring's pulsing temptations.

Pale tight redness of the fruit and silky skins
crack between my teeth.

I drift upon you in the molded creams
which pour forth from tender soils.

Fields of Wheat

Looking upon the cowering fields of wheat,
each strand and fiber sulks beneath the pressing wind.

Tracing my fingers along, I drift my thoughts
to the sweet scents of your hair
which blooms full as your delicate, cool skin
sitting as the nearby apple groves, ripe and thin to the touch.

I pause by the slicing creek.
Your moisture grooms heavy beneath my chest.

I gather a few leaves of the maple tree.
My mouth sweetens to the touch.
Damp, I soothe the burn of your tempest and groin.
Here, I am alive in flavors which tremble through
with the valleys spices, settled upon my tongue.

Autumn Flowers

I stand by the chill of your satin gown.
In a dash, I release heavy breath upon your pale shoulders.

You trace a single finger along my shivering arm;
beneath us, the flowers of deep fall pull
in quivering surrender.

By the thick of night, I watch as your full lips
gasp to the gloat of the moon.

Lost

The pond drew small waves from the toss of the wind.
Her reflection danced from edge to the slickness of edge.

Her pale glazed flesh, I spoke in riddles into her soft ears.

With the touch of her fragile hands
To the blitz of my crooning groin,
I spoke of the wavering kelp which longed to touch
The wince of our face and the dance of our fingers.

~

Walking home, I listened in the clamor of the clouding fog
Which gasped as the thinnest cloth swabbing in sheets
Of the sky which gripped us tight.

I touched her on the mouth and lost the path we walked.

March, 2018

The frosted edge, fanned into quiet
recession with the sweep of the sun,
softened the soils which returned to the
lusty forest, spreads of moisture.

I placed the palms of my hands upon the prisms
of her gleaming waist and abdomen, dancing flesh
beneath the tremor of my saucing mouth, fingers roamed.

I open the majesty of her thighs, tender
and alone in the palest white.
I smell the life of the earth as patches of
snow wilt and bleed a serum
crawling to the roots, now snarling in return.

Watching you as life finds bounty, from finger to finger,
from palm to palm.

By the sauces of afternoon, I witness
the shaking bloom of your hair
as I gesture a deepness and delve into the woods.

Gardener

Weeds soaked each pouch of grass.
Slipped from the earth, I pinched, snipped
with the grip of my finger and the plump
grapple of my heavy thumb.

The drenching sun drew saps and beads
along the exploits of my neck and shuffling shoulder.

Pausing in a thick thirst, I drank
the crisp water which seasoned the meadow.

As the brook threaded it's way,
I peered into the rolling hills, mounded with the moss
covered rocks.

I rubbed my neck and made my way home.

A Distance from Summer

The bloom carried in currents.
Yellow pollens scattered as the shade of melting butters.

Gingerly, the seeds filled the dormancy
of my lungs and mouth.
Thinking of the slow gestures of her
dampened me in a sweat which shook and sulked
across the postures of my quivering body.

Looking upon the gentle gathering of trees,
the elm, oak, and maple, enticed the gasping winds.

Every risen root fell beneath me as a crowd
of bones aching to the tamp of my foot.

Here I placed the last breath of you as the moans
of Autumn flickered through the trees
and pooled about my throat-
alive the chalks of this season.

Mumbling Voices

Standing by the pulse of this slicing river,
I hear the voices of my ancestors now thrown in powders
upon the breath of morning, softly
treading in the lowest cloud.

The mud caked to my shoes tell tales
of what once hung as flesh and now sulk to the earth.

Holding the frailty of her hand, I
smiled and placed my being
so swiftly upon her, dancing in paints she spoke of reward.

Edging away from the water,
we drifted into the cleaved trail.

This antiquated home wrapped as a wooden sheet
born of ply and log, standing strong on the mumbling earth.

Baking in Breads

Breads swam in prowling heat, I watched the rise
penetrate through the afternoon.

Wearing the last of my t-shirts, I broom
upon the dampness in the air.
Your breasts tug beneath the cottons and opened my
mouth to her fabric, born of hem and stitch.

~

I smiled upon your doughs which pulled sweats
from the heat, roaming across the kitchen
and all it's dampness.

Now evening, I could smell the yeasts
scatter across the heavy house.
I called your name in a quiet hush.

Elm Leaf

The last star at morning gently faded.
The fog lifted and the mist remained, recalling
a closeness with the somber earth.

I felt the bones and skin, quiet beneath
the coarseness of my pulsing hands.

Walking past an iced pond, floating in chips,
I felt the humid breath of you
pour in cylinders from my mouth.

I look into the tree lined pasture and notice
a single leaf rest upon the great elm.

In a brief moment, the mists fell to the frosted grasses,
all groom and landed soft.

Follow

You walk with me through each room of the house.
I feel the coolness of the wooden floor
as the candles whimper and dance to the draft.

By vanity and sulking cloth, I soaked in your
delicate scents which pull as an open breeze-
this clever gale on this open field

which I peer upon when gazing through the cracked
enticing window.

You come to me in vapors as the field
and all it's stillness defy every breath of you.

Yet, I pull you in my presence, the shake
of my weary legs and buckle of my neck and shoulders.

As the gift of each trembling moment,
I pull you within me.

Grove

The apple grove boasted of it's redness
and softly flickered and tugged with
the haunt of the silent wind.

I placed the fleshy pulp in the cave of my mouth
as teeth snapped heavily upon the wine colored film.

Motioning for her, she threaded with the most patient touch
and I felt the valleys of my shoulder and back posture
soothingly with the draping wind.

~

I crooned for the mouth of her with the snip of each pie.

With a sweet breath, I looked upon her
as the sun frolicked through each silk
thread of her auburn hair.

Into the grip of her moist fingers, I lulled
for a taste of her quivering lips.

Marinade

I look to the east and I lather in pinks and purple dressings.
Looking to the west, darkness coats as a heavy paint,
cloaks in the silence of the blackness.

I stand by this cove and breath perfumes of the gentle
ocean, tonight's gentle ocean.

I fill my lungs with the salts of a sultry marinade.
With every step, I come closer to you.

Memorial Day, 2017

She gestured with her touch, a soft moss
Groomed upon a stone which stood still
And silent against the wind.

I looked at her as the tongue of my mouth grew dry
With the scouring breeze blown in the heavy drafty
Season.

I felt the ices of her eyes fragment across me.
She prayed in an absence and shook near the oak wood tree,
Only to bush and filter along the skies endless winds.

Last Evening in the Forest

I rest by this pond, bloomed full in the greenest kelp.
Maples undress as I peer to the threads, thinning clouds.

I uncover my hands from the pockets of my coat;
I touch my parched lips as the cool rain taps upon me.

Leaves tumble and dance through this forest,
enticing each footstep I depressed, arriving at this marvel.

Nearby, a gathering of ferns waves to me
as a majestic worship to the glimmering sun,

So alive through these damp clamoring branches.
Somewhere in this hour of evening,

the slender fog drips to the richest soil of these
towering woods.

Dreaming by moonlight, I descend.

Resting

The fields, host pale lemon grass
and offer both clover and the onion sprout.

Trim and lined, each evergreen stands guard as a sentinel.
Each pine cone thuds the earth in memorandum.

I absorb the still and silent soils beneath each tender foot.

By evening, soon nightfall, the winds cool
the green linens of the meadow.

I adhere to the approaching storm and
use the dryness of my eager body
to gather water pellets about my mouth and lips.

I feel the rattle of my bones and the drip of my marrow
as I rest by pasture and tree.

Listening to Seagulls

The shadowed contours of your soft, soothing face
Settled upon me as I sank beneath you.

Absorbing the cushions of your flowery breasts,
I wavered above in goblets from which I feed.

I touched the ocean waves which gathered around each
curve of your waist.

In rhythms, your foams of the inlet, so close to the sea,
spread across my abdomen, pulled my groin as a buoy.

Lost quietly in the waters,

I reached your mouth with finger and thumb.
Here, I heard the seagulls cry.

Flesh and Fog

The clouds fell to the earth in robes.

Falling tender to the search of the acorn
holding dear each tamping oak.

Looking upon the gasping winds, a blossom
and bud scampered along the pathways edge.

I slowly recall your touch and mourn
with each swimming layer of fleshing fog.

Slumber

Here, this gash of the earth washed along in froth and foam.

Treading my fingers, I relished in the milks of the most
distant mother, mourning the absence
of a finely groomed Fall.

When I released the grip of my calloused palm,
the ices slipped across in pirouettes.

Coveting the frosted arms of the snowbank,
above, the crows neighbored and sang so sweetly.

By the end of Winter, I stood and walked my way home
through the pulsing rhythms of Spring.

Patiently Awaiting

You kneel above me as your lips quiver
Somberly in the pounding rain.

The absence of your powdered, malted breasts
Deepen me further as I breathe with the passing wind.

I empty into you in plasmas
Which uproot with the cultivation of Spring.

I soothe the fallen seed and the tender mulch.

I wrap across your pale shoulders as the drenching
Breeze gathers in a hush.

Most eager I await your term
Where the chill of your body dampens nearest mine.

Drought

The verbs brought moisture to the crimped, dry fields.

She asked why the rain abandoned

and she asked why the trees shred the
leaves as an ancient book

shreds parchment.

By nightfall, the skies opened in a puncture

where the teardrops sop and cream upon the meadow.

By the deep of midnight, she rest by the towering tree

and kissed swoons upon the lips.

Spring Visitation

The lawn filtered to a pathway, rubbled rocks and pebbles
which stretched along the emerald hills.

I walked for a time, then paused
to thicken my lungs with a slight frost,

peppering the shadowed reach of the trees.

~

With a closure of my eyes and a tremor
pounding beneath both coat and shirt

I stand and witness the paleness of your nestled bed.
Drifting, I smell the perfumes and powders

of your swollen breasts which gather pulses
from soil to the dancing breeze.

~

I smile between the gasping approach of a tender rain.

Gently, I hear you moan, majestic as thunder.

Stillness of the Water

Today, the lake spent several hours
maintaining a somber silence.
Ridged, the roots and shucks of the bamboo
made smooth gestures to the sun, spreading in oils
of the shoreline sunflowers, quivering to each slight breeze.

~

She swam in the nakedness of the afternoon.

I watched the rivets of seeping water caress
each sculpted curve,
from breast to the damp sheets along her abdomen.

~

Looking above, the blackbird and the mourning dove
shook through the stillness of the sky.

A moment later, the seeds of the pines
edge vanished to the vastness.

Fig

Figs rested in the nooks of my mouth.
Each flicker and dribble soothed their way
along my cheek and lips.

In the slight motion of this creviced posture,
I proclaim to her roaming legs and groom
of her thighs where barleys roam by the most
tender gash of the earth.

Into the thick blankets of nights blackest hour,
I slept in her moistest fields where valleys drain
each pouring river and stream.

By Pond

The vine coiled from root to open spread,
Canvas of the dried wood, dried tree.

Peering warmly into the woods, I felt
the cool wrap of your arms soothe around me.

~

We walked, hiking into the deep greens
and arrived at the pensive pond,
filled with kelp, tadpoles and mossy rocks.

I placed my lips upon your painted lips.

We sat and watched the ruffling, robust leaves
thread across the forest floor.

Your hand slipped into mine.
By midday, sun tethered through the treetops.

Lakes Edge

The lake swallowed the rain in small dancing gems.
Standing by the shoreline, I smelled the crisp water
and the surrounding spreads of the earth
which gifted minerals as the waving winds tumbled.

I held the reaching arm of the spruce,
leaned gently and calm.

The canvased greens soaked in a tender cascade.
I loafed loose along the needled floor.

Gestures

I sank the proding gab of my fingers and palm
well into the earth where she slept.

Quiet Spring morning, the cleanliness of the rain
made almost silent vows with the mud and minerals,
packed upon you as you lay.

I tore softly in mumbling verbs which strode
across the tissues of the heavy air.

I returned to the slithering path which lead me to my home.

I sulked my way to the bedroom where particle and dust
drafted about the room across sheet and pillow.

The heat pipes choked as I touched you in gestures.
So soon, I will slumber.

End of Day

The silk blue sky weaned the buttery yoke
with the lift of the slim clouds, dampness
of a lofting linen.

I spoke into the breath of morning
as humid vapors streamed from the tongue and jaw
of my mouth.

~

Looking upon you, I stared at the cresting evergreens
which brag of your softness and their eager roots.

~

When the soft, soothing drizzle patted upon the tender grass,
I awoke and swam in the sweats of my bed
and slithered about the coolness of my heavy down pillow.

~

Later that day, I sank my hands into the muds of the earth.

Warmth of the Sun

There lay a garment on the chipped wooden floor.
I peer through the bedroom window
near the standing mirror which tossed glimmering fragments
across the endless space from where you once lay.

Gathering the abandoned cloth, I spread
in the scents of you as the flickering dusts coveted
my face and burning mouth.

Tenderly, I gathered my things and hike
deeply into the woods, searching for you.

By midday, the sun croons as a globe and dances upon us
near meadow and grove.

Resurrection

The grape hyacinth scampered across the forest floor.
A warm breeze broomed their way to
the full white azalea bush.

Alone, each puckering mineral of mulch rose
in this resurrection of moist soil, alive beneath the fine
groomed air, pulled and tugged the drifting petal
rested by the fallen leaf.

I can feel my shoes deepen to the earth.
Pausing by the roadway, I looked in
abundance to the pounding
-Summer sun.

Thinking of You after a Rainstorm

The fields were lusty and dry.
Then the rain came.
Pounding in battalions, the earth mourned it's loss
and gathered the ripest of muds.

Stones sizzled to the smokey air, fumes.

I stood so lucid on the wooden deck.
Softly, I smelled the earth and thought of you
standing gently beside me.

Clouds darkened and swarmed the trembling sky.
From here, I could taste your neck, nape and nave.

By nightfall, the earth grew cool
And loosened a slithering breath of humid air.

I walked through the open meadow.

Soft Rain

Whipping through the open air,
the bells rang,
pulsing my ears in a rhythm which gripped
and malted the fragrance of my whispering flesh.

I walked to you on the weed filled
cracks of the winding sidewalk.

I mulled across your breasts as they filled
each fabric and pouch.

The soft rain riddled the earth and road,
I felt the steam as if rising from my tightening skin.

By night, I watched the candle seep in waxes.
I felt the dryness of my mouth waver
as you faded beyond.

Settling Dust

Midnight and the northern gales swept the pollens
and spread the dust of the earth as I stood
silent on the patio, nursing the blackest coffee.

⁓

Heavy blues trimmed along the horizon
as the stars glinted the freckles roaming
across your chest and breasts.

You have returned as sweet marrow to the soil.
Hundreds of neighboring scents rose.
Each flower and mushroom patch aroused in soft scents.

I lay the cheek of my face to the wet sobbing grass
where you speak of tender grooming. The notions
of renewal grip me in my crimping palm.

I recall how you once would bring sweat
to the linens of our bed.
Now I sleep in the cool draft of the room.
The dust has settled and the plump gloat of the moon
-surrendered.

Crackling Night

The slow moving creek melded in dark
greens and buttery yellows.
The soft air tunneled through my hair,
Dancing upon the sting of my face.

I looked to the plump sky.
The blackbirds held each branch a treasure.

I smelled you as the fragrant dust of the dashing leaves
Scuffled across the ground.

I wept as you faded into the crackling night,
Both legs and arms of the towering trees.

Coveted Clays

Tan dusts cracked along the clays of this abandoned earth.

Now thick in the afternoon, the wind bloomed
and each quiet seedling slid scampered along.

I stood still and pulled these scents across the bounty
of my torso and face.

The bones were countless as they coveted the clay grip,
tangled roots motionless since last Spring.

I walked far, deep into this place
and heard her moan upon the spartic winds.

Tumble and Dance

The creek water, rich in pebble and kelp,
sliced fluid as solvents
while I stood so close
watching the elm leaves carry.

I tasted the moisture in the air.
I could recall, her hand tucked into mine,
the winds from a most northern point
seduced me to the surrounding thickness of a heavy wood.

Within a draft, I absorbed her through each
pore of my chilled skin.

When I peered upon the ground, I
watched the loose leaves tumble in a dance.

How sweetly you poured across me.

Dreamed

I bathed in the Summer draft,
slippery damp winds trellised through my hair
and shook the stance of my bones.

I laid upon moss covered rock, smooth and flat.
Closing my eyes, she draped beside me
as I whimpered to her cheeks and painted lips.

So sweetly, she placed my spinning head
upon the flowery scent of her breasts.
I shook into the breathing sky, dreamed of the lilac
-her trembling thighs.

When morning jousted across me,
I weakened to the dash of soft light and I
found peace on this smooth moss covered rock.

Waiting a Year

Once, I tasted her in sauces glazed
across both shoulder and neck.
She filled me in aromas, spices permeating from her
soft, creamy skin.

About a year ago, this Spring, she left, dissolved to the breeze.
I stand so still, watching the lilies breed upon lilies.
When the crust of the earth swarms into
the soon approaching muds

I cleanse with these buds, ripe as the
blemishes upon your skin.

Your flavors suckle both flower and
dewdrops on the wiry weeds.

Morning Dream

Fine threads of your silky hair,
full and cascading down your shoulders,
fill the room in fine fragrance and spices.

I motioned to you as the freshest rain
on a sweet Spring morning
I watched the dewdrops sit, set, and tremble
across the sloping curves of your neck.

Slowly, I absorbed into the press
of your full, blossomed breasts.

Waking to the fog and steam,
I watched as you dissipated into the heavy
glint of sunshine,
prancing through the quiet morning spread.

From Spring to Spring

I awoke, captured by the faint light of morning.
Sweet water perched on the windowpane, sulked in streams
of drizzling beads.

With quiet recollection, she danced about the room,
permeating a fragrant lingering draft, from wall to wall,
floor to ceiling.

Now, Spring hushed across me.
As she fled to the earth, last Spring,
she crowds my stinging flesh in riddling vapors.

I open my mouth to the breath of this seasonal aroma
and I hear the floorboards creak in rejuvination.

I recall the soft press of her feet as they would slightly
tamp the hardwood floor.

In a gasp, I lift my mouth ajar.
I pull each drifting scent into the pulse of my veins.

Picnic

With wind dancing across the woodland pond,
hair, full as the soothing kelp, washed
into the once still waters.

The closeness of the trembling willow tree
offered in slowness and quiet.

As she dripped from the green waters,
I listened to the opening breeze
climb the full nakedness of her body.

After Nightfall into Deep of Morning

The broad window, closed with drapes, when pulled open
sulked as the stretch of your arms
through silk and satin sleeves.

The glisten of sun threaded about the room
as I lay still and watched you undress. I weaned,

pulled from the bareness of you pale, white breasts
and faded to the dusty fragment of daylight.

With the window open and freshness
pouncing around the quiet room,
I trembled to the rising scents of garden and grass.

Soothingly, I returned my posture to the mulch and soils
from which I roam.

Waiting in the Evergreen

I surf the treetops of this evergreen forest.
In a snap, the pine cones bury into the pine needle bed.
So gently, I caress the winding sprawl of the stream
dug from beneath the mountainous spring.

Thinking of you, I thicken into the soft blues
of the drifting sky.

With the hush of a moment's thought,
I cannot find you.
Swiftly, I scour the dampening earth
as the rain taps the quiet bed, waiting.

Breath

On this once silent earth, I hear you whimper
as I cross with the bareness of my feet.

I hook my toes to the quiver of the beginning rain.
The sods of this open field undress with your tapping winds.

As you return to the threading tears
flinched with the opening sky,

I find your scents liven with the stroke of the lilac
and sweeten upon the patch of mint.

~

I search the forest, field, and meadow as you
tightly thicken to the soft earth.

With the deepest breath, slowly I find you.

Country Walking

Her mouth was the freshness of an open meadow.
Rich, smooth, and restless as the tumbling grass.

Her breasts rolled as the gentle hills,
soaked in the quiet rains.

~

Gingerly, I walked the valley
and solemnly, I thought of your lips, tenderly painted.

When I reached the summit of your smile and aspect,
I felt the wind tug across my chest and face.

~

I lean along the basin of the tree, a quiet spruce,
I feel your arms wrap around me.

Searching

Through the dense green of thicket
shrouded in the clamoring woods,
I heard your voice tremble with the partnering trees.
Soothing, the scampering leaves nestled for you,
calmly resting as a bed.

The motherly sky opened as a blouse and dampened
the earth and all it's soft and pebbled soil as a warming breast.

I shunned the quiet nights
as I roamed and searched for your quivering belly,
soft as the pastures courting the trees edge.

By the deepest night,
I felt the flavors of a pattering rain.

Somber, the mask of the black bleeding sky sulked.
I so quickly, then fell into you.

Fondling Quartz

A stretch of quartz gathered jettison from the riverbed.
With a tug and pull,
I turned and faced the glamor of the prowl of the sun.

So sweetly, I placed the rock in the nest of my hand.

As you swept across in the spread of an afternoon wind,
I tossed the glazed rock into the thick
swim of the rolling stream.

In a slow walk home,
I looked to the heavy sky, trembling with rain and asked
you when we can touch in the pouring river?

I smiled and turned away, slowly.

Resting by the Stream

After we touched, hand to hand and lips to lips,
I looked upon the blossoming trees and felt the velvet
winds as they threaded through my coarse, gray beard.

Gently, I knelt to the river.
I swabbed the cool breeze from channel to rapids
onto the slanted side of my face.

It was then that you trembled upon me
with the coiling waters.

In a rhythmic dance, I loosened your silk finished clothes.
By the slant of morning, I walked the streams edge
and found you resting in the earth, as I left you years ago.

Roaming with Nightfall

Cherry stained cabinets and shelves,
held the spices, teas, and flour,
powdered as were your fragrant breasts.

I trimmed off the dust and my sight of you vanished
as the lingering scents you held so smoothly in your hair.

I stood, crossed my arms and held you, wrapped in the
thick of my arms.

~

With approaching nightfall, you removed, resolved
and quietly disappeared.

~

Outside, I heard the crows rambling in a throated tenseness.

Each nestling beak fed upon the seeds
of the meadow and creek
which sliced it's way through the hills where you roam.

Asleep by the Ocean's Cove

Her hair, full as fields of barley, soothed
across her pale and tender shoulders.
Saps spread as a hidden cove which held the richness
of a perfectly timed flood, the silky shores.

I absorbed into you.
I heard the creak and moan of your softening bones
which took to the air in a dusty flight.

Now, at the dancing pearl beads of morning,
I walked through your garden and wisped
upon the ashes you the soft air once tossed and gripped.

So near to the rippling water where you would bathe,
I hooked my toes into the soot where you sleep.

Into my Lungs

Quietly, leaves fell and cushioned to the fragrant Spring soil.

Gathering a few in the tender grip of my hand, I pulled
them to the edge of my face and
breathed the remnanta of you
into my lungs.

~

When you were young, I was young.

I felt the muscles of my legs kick through the dusty dirt
which settled only to return to the drafty air
in blossoms of the nearby seeds and pollens.

~

With tight recollection, I dampened to you in whispers.

The forest stretched as a maze. Jigsaws peppered the crunch
of the dry timbered floor.
I reached my eyes to the swelling
descent of the pods and buds
and crooned to you of the softest growth.

A Place of Light and Rest

I spent my afternoon gazing loosely
across the spread stones, standing as a guardian.

The meadow, heavy greens, fluttered as a contribution.
Grass whispered silently as they rose in minerals
from the soil and bedded mulch.

Into the distance, the sparse clouds lifted
along the rim of the crevice and peak of the mountain.

With recollection, I dream swiftly of the pouring creek.
Here we would lay and drift among each other,
with touch and loose fitting clothes.

Now you have deepened in this emerald valley.
I long to kiss your trembling face once more.

Vanish

She slouched upon the meadow in gravities,
Warm air and cool to the touch.

I stood silent, watching her sink to the soil,
A richness which rests so deeply in the earth.

The December sun tooled soft, the stretching clouds
Spread as a thin cotton cloth.

~

I returned in ices, grooming through the frosty caps
Which stroked across the meadow and scattered pines;

Home now, I warm as each finger, each limb, and groin
Burns with the sting of a Winter's gloat.

Soothingly, I feel the pulses of her quivering abdomen,
I feel the haunt of her vapors as swift, she vanishes.

Night I Covet

Now nightfall triumphs in heavy blues
and thick black ribbons.

Sleek, wet drips of evening dewdrops
prepare and covet my toes, arms, and stiff legs.

I come to you in the trembling wind,
which carries my scent to far off mountains
and distant lakes.

Open me to your lungs and wrap me
across your thirsting face.

I am the sap of the maple tree and the rippling waters
of each creek and brook.

Together, we will travel from soil bed to soil bed
from purring stream to gathering trees, heavy this forest.

> So near, I hear the sobbing ocean.
> I gather my boots and continue on…

Pebble

As a young girl
you would gather small pebbles
and lay them on the calm patio table
which threw glimpses of sun, dancing
across your small, tender face.

I recall the sun was dripping in orange and warm pink.

Holding your hand,
we walk the grass filled lawn. We stopped
and gathered a few more.

Morning Time

I look to the spread of the warm early sun;
squinting, I see the hazy lemon of the thin horizon.

The blues and tender white clouds roamed as a gown,
swooping down to the dusty earth.

There rests satin shades upon the forest floor;
ferns which confront with each tickle and wave.

Oceans of tepid, thick air searches for harbor,
she suckles the pollens, casting aside.

Age

Slowly, there threshed voices through the trees.
I moved to the edge of the rock chipped path
and listened to every sound.

In a moment, I was asked to enter this full, plentiful
forest.

Now, I am lost. Cleverly I speak to
the oak, elm, and sycamore.

Lime Green

As the lime green buds which swelled to the twig, I smiled against the mild gusts of breeze,

I thought of you with tossed shirts and pale fumbling breasts. Passages of cool morning surrendered through each pinch of shirt and skirt.

I found myself tucked and fallen into you.

Toward Mountains Peak

I softly held her hand and dripped in flavors
which aroused my chest and tempered
both tongue and groin.

Into the distance,
fog trimmed the mountain peak.

I recall her touch as we walked this trail.

Seeds

Your full hair slouched black
as the seed of an apple, burrowing against pale flesh.

When you gather a smile,
I am witness to the thin, calm, softness of your mouth.
Tender parting and I warmly blush.

Tomorrow, I will empty the bees of their honey.

Sweet scents of your flowered dress;
I have nothing more to give.

Groaning Lilacs

When the weather rode a warmer path,
I smelled the perfumes of your hair.

Softness of your pale, quiet flesh opened
to me as the lilac bush, groaning for a quivering rain.

Now heavy Winter,
I cannot find you. Your scent left with the scampering breeze.

Nightfall

The trim fracture, purples and indigos, sank to the horizon.
My tender eyes watched as the shadow dredged
the earth in heavy inks.

I looked to the breads of the sky,
the moon wrapped as a cocoon.

Listening to noises of meadow and river,
I heard humming, each breath of every plant.

Upon these Hills

The mountain perched upon masses of sacred earth.

I stood from this valley, witness to white glazed
fangs which gnashed the sky.

Thin air, hawks groomed the heavens
with claw and beak, searching
for the delicate and frail.

Watching the clouds spread slim like gauze, I
felt the hot butters of my chest
tear through my veins and suckle the grip of my lips.

~

I recall how we would roam these hills
and steep in wonder of the great mountain,
shredding the sky.

Leaving, I heard the voices from the richest soil
Moan of the dusts parted from their deepened bones.

Eclipse

Smoke slithered across the emerald grass.
I stepped against each slippery blade.

Your footprints turned to the west as mine
held greedy to the east.

The sun fastened to the moon.

After a Rest in Avalon

The wind skirted the ocean. I can hear her
with beats of her taught brine drum.

The kelp danced as the foamed white caps
made tangled love.

Into the cove they rest. Each shell seeking a restful home.
Tossed back to their origin
which took countless years baking under the creamy pink
and slouching purple sky.

I walk the sanded streets and breathed.

These dunes are precious breads which soften my feet.

Cloudy Morning

Your breath,
smoky fog on a slippery grass pasture,
washes across me.

So tender,
I slumber against the warmth of your gentle breast,
I sulk to the haze between our mouths.

Touching the misty flesh
upon your pale white abdomen,
I shake to the shadowy field which

softens juice and dew shuddering on the heaviest weeds.
By morning, the clouds lift.

Shattered Woods

Lusty air swims across me, hair blown full-
sun taps through the treetops.

I lost my path.
I rest so deeply here in these brown and yellow woods.

By night, I lay my windblown head upon the mosses.
I can hear the insect chant their hymns.
Awake, the sun flickers and I quietly step
along these broken paths.

Traveling East

The iced, frothy creek poured out of the mountain,
where chipped rock, splintered log and branch held the bones
of this falling vein, inviting upon the soil.

I stood along a valleys peak.
Summer alive and the rain smashed
through channel and rapids.
Creeping slow along the water's edge,
I took a heavy drink,
razors down mouth and throat.

Now in meadows bloomed and full, I
dipped my thick fingers about pollen and saps.
I look east to the rising sun,
notice an oak loosening acorns.

I stop and rest, still thirsty.

Distant Fires

Awakened to the howl and cloak of nights chill;
I could see the dust gleam where she once lay.

Following the scent of her soft, full, red hair-
all was gone, her bag, blouse and skirt.

~

Listening to the preach of the wind,
I walked to the grotto.
Smoke rose in the distance.
Fires burning in the depth of night.

Spending Time Alone by the River

I kneel by the softness of the river.
It pulses bloods which pour through my veins.

Nearby, I watch as the puckering buds
lean to the splashing sun.

Roaming through my face and hair,

I cleanse by touch of heat and smooth
by washing my leathered and crimping skin.

The endlessness of dancing water,
I wade, knee deep, through the quickest pastures.

By midday, I can witness the grasses wave
and laugh with the prowl of the most tender breeze.

By end of day, I walk home, defeated by the thick
inks which cloak the sky.

Bedtime Stories

I pressed my lips upon the thin tremble of your lips,
I quivered in nocturnes, slippery along the linens.

So tender, the pasture of your abdomen told tales
of the barley and wheat which roamed thick
through the Pennsylvania landscape.

The dance of your flickering eyes took flight,
speaking of the blackbird whom slung across the gray
of the Wintery skyline.

Soft and smooth as eager silks, your breasts
told of the threaded foam which cascade
across the white rivers and all it's bloom.

As I fell to the heavy slumber of night,
I whispered upon the edge of her ear
and ushered verbs of the roaming treetops
which flood the prowling forest floor.

Teardrops

Teardrops ran across your tender cheeks,
dispersed along the thinness of your lips.

Cleverly, the wind threaded your hair.
Salted sweat gathered against your temples and
moistened your soft, pale neckline.

I placed a petal, lost from its root and stem, against
your arm and watched as the sun slipped across the horizon.

Gripped in the Fog

Through the field, fog gathered smoke
circling my legs and lifting in patches
only to depress again. They washed upon me.

The grass clung to my denim and shoes,
gathering clippings.

I thought of you and smelled the richness
of your hair.
The scent of you as I wandered lost, I felt
the chilled grip of your delicate hands
with each step.

Chestnuts and Apricots

I watch as the frailty of your thin hands
carried the brown chestnuts, clung
in the pouch of your palm.

Soft, the apricots of your pulsing flesh
threw scents of sandalwood, creeping about the room.

As I placed the thickness of my hands
across your warm lips,

I felt the breeze from your mouth
tangle me in rhythms.

Fire Pit

Now, Spring and the grass flushed emeralds
tossed in the breath of morning.

Gathering wood for the fire, I could sense
the distant sun as it dripped
shade after shade of tender pinks.

The dewdrops, flickering white, smoothed along
my mouth as I placed the mint leaves against my tongue.

Hours later, I watched the robins roam the field,
taking flight moments later.

I heard the breeze whisper across my pale skin.
The clouds were beginning to lift.

Alone

I could smell the soil upon you,
quiet minerals and decay of marrow and bone.

The stone cools the back of my neck and chills my head.
Slouching, I lean back in curves.
Tenderly, I drift to a soft sleep.

When I awaken, the thick moon spread
across the crawling sky.

Curving Bones

The curve of my bones
edge their way to your soft frame,
so tender we collide in the press
gentle down and quilt.

~

Here, in the sweet of morning,
I feel my trembling fingers and thumbs.

Your eager mouth slips
as the ponds of forest deep.

A few days later,
I pluck the oak leaf from the quivering pond
and softly walk away.

Valley Invites

The trail swept through generous hills.
Both plants and shrubs waved me along,
- breath of the countryside.

I slowly lay to the rocks and quiet dirt,
dust of earth danced across my face.

~

I looked to the sycamore where we touched last Spring.

The draft caroused across me. Gathering your scents,
the valley grew so inviting.

Winter Defeat

In the thick of warmth, a dancing
flash of sun while the wind shook across tree leaves
and settled the puddled rain, cupped every leaf.

I held the flickering moisture of the morning,
drizzling upon my shoulders as the trees swayed.

~

By night, the day had drifted in endless
Hazy columns. Purging across the thin
horizon, I stood and walked through the cool
dampness of cloaked night.

~

By midnight, I thrust in spreads along the drifting
wind which coated the earth. This chill coiled through
as youthful Spring upon my skin.

The mountains groomed the soft gray clouds.
I stood close to the tremble of my window.
By cliff and rocky face, Winter snarled defeat.

Going Home

Hills, alive in green of cascading pines,
ushered forth a moist and rich spice.

I leaned against the tree, riddled in barks. I thought of the
hidden saps as the naked wind bloomed.

I recalled the way she would slither out of her skirt.
I recalled how she unbuttoned her blouse -as the drifting sky.

Reaching into the pouch of my jacket
I removed a smoke which lingered to leaf and tree branch.

Watching the valley, dripping in fog,
so slow it lifted.

I stood by spruce and chattering limbs.
The trail led home and I scampered fast.

I filled my lungs with the scent of her.

By the Ocean

Her mouth was silent, soft as she slept.
Gently, I threaded my fingers along her cascading hair,
watching the paleness eager skin.

I laid my head, temples, against her abdomen.

Listening to the wild ocean, crashing and crumbling waves,
each window held splatters of brine.

In the darkest moment of the evening, I shift
to the hidden breath beneath her breasts.

Childhood Dreaming

The river swelled along the bank and buried the scattered
rocks beneath grassy mud.

Slouched against this moss covered log,
I lift my torso and arms to the cool dance of morning air.

Looking to the tender forest,
I heard the moans of the bark threaded along trees

and the bones which slept in the heavy, rich earth.

When I found the thin trail deepening
into the breads of the softest foggy mist,

the woods surrounded me. I was lost.
With this ancient trail beneath my heavy feet,

I wandered into a distant realm, dreaming.

Walk along the Beach

She came to me in vanilla of her soft skin.
I roamed across her as the storm dredging
the ocean, endlessly thick.

Looking upon her thin lips
slithered forth a humid breath-
jousting in soft spices.

My feet sulked through the sands and foams
upon my feet and calves.

She broomed by in a salty breeze-
I softened as a swabbed cocoon,
tender in the press of coming moonlight.

Birds at Play

Fingers trellised down the slopes of my shoulders.
I shook and purred glazes from my mouth.

~

Quick, I stood and dressed as the late Autumn rain slapped
heavy against the brick home, windows.

Walking the spine of the hazed, misty road,
I felt the vapors rise from my neck and scalp.

~

In the fracture of a moment, the rain ceased.
A flock of blackbirds roamed at play.

Remembrance During a Snowy Night

Sheets of white stretched,
groomed beneath the splashing sun.

I stood upon the neighboring road, glanced
to the mounds, carpeted snows.

Crisp Winter air sliced through me.

~

Now, resting within the home, iron stove-
edge to edge, my skin crept in needles.

The wind slapped and howled along the walls.
I glanced to her robe and scents drifted across me.

~

Weighed in the tug and pull of her, I
sulked so distant, a touch, long ago,
wrestled me in the fabrics she tenderly wore.

Dreamt by Moonlight

Moving as a tender feline, she roamed by satin,
opened breath slithering through the room.

Creams pressed, warm breads sauntered their way
through the draft, alive this painted mouth.

~

I left, soaked the moonlit hours.

Asleep this gathering of trees peppered me in leaves-
tickling tired skin, her heavy scent slung,
entered caverns of my chest.

~

By morning, I awoke to the dancing sun.
I gathered both sting and harvest
of the thickest of dreams.

Tangerine Sky

Looking at the lilac bush,
skies gray brood with each darkened cloud.

I snapped the brown buds with finger and thumb.
Then, tossed aside to the still, yet softly threaded earth.

With the flash of an electric light, I felt the sting
of needling raindrops skewer to each edge of my flesh.

~

Days later, the lilac softened and grew
as the sky passed in tangerines.

I threw a swift look and the sun swept
by pillowing clouds.

Voice of the Woods

The oak tree spoke in voices
of a trembling hollow,
pounding through the woods.

Scattered and splintered, quick shaves
of the bark rest upon the leafy floor.

From limb and branch,
echoes of a temperate bloom,

-faded in grays.

Stopping by the riverside, I washed the edge
and curve of my grounded face.

By morning, I slipped through the passages
of a slouching woods.

Seductively, the sun fell against
each grain and chip.

Near

As the shadows grew across angles and drifts
of my face, body, and hands, I walked
through a moist pasture,
so awake.

The powders of pollens and pods
Pressed to the midday air.

Soothing Ferns

The lightly wooded pasture grew saplings
which spoke of their staffs, leaning upon the quiet earth.

In a flickering twitch, ferns soothed the crusted bark
and opened a softness to the panting breath of wind.

During the dampest of mornings,
soil and moss lay as a canvas upon their gentle
touch. Each dew drop kissed in return.

I gave my pulse
from the depth of lung and throat.

Silky air funneled through my chilled mouth
and mixed perfect with the threads of fog-

climbing across the green buds, giving voice
to the approach of temperate visions
where all will bloom thick and full.

River Curves through Mist

The roots of the sky
hung in haze and vapors, licking grass fields-
stretching to the river.

~

Walking across, I felt the crunch of stiff
blades weep beneath my heavy boots.

At riverside, grooming patterns of wind
soothed their way along the rolling
sauces -white capped.

~

With a moan of the wind,
The sullen clouds sank.

I turned my path and followed the bending
curves of the river.

Softly, I followed the smoke of the crouching sky.

Waiting on the Crow

Dark ash, the smokey clouds slithered
across the gently waving lake.

I stood on the shoreline, watching the boats
throw orange humming lights from edge to edge.

Now, in the depth of night, the rippling splashes
moistened pebble and grass.

Her breath lent trickling perfumes
into the shrug of my chest and groin.

~

I returned a day later.
The ash was gone and the lights
fed upon the delicacies of heavy evening.

The water returned.
The crow passed overhead and I thought of her.

When the Mist Settles

Rain mumbled as it struck the asphalt and sidewalk.
Running in rivets, pooling along the creviced
concrete, I watched as the weeds rejoiced.

The evergreens flickered their needled hoods,
shaking loose pine cones which patted upon damp earth.

Maples fed the pulses of their hidden saps,
coating their soil and dreaming of their roots.

Pulps of the red berry, born of the holly bush,
tapped against the cool ground.

I turned to the clever woods, roaming and searching.

By morning, the rain ceased.
By morning, the mist had settled.

As Light Beckons

Minerals of the soil gasped beneath my naked feet.
Toes warm and sunk,
I fed my way through the each spread of the soft garden.

The plants, alive in greens and whites, licked their
breath from clover to mint patch
-puckering draft.

Kneeling adjacent to the heavy bay windows,
flickering light to the sleek, hush of the French doors,
the light from within the silent home
danced across my eyes and face.

Now, looking to the surface of each cloud,
I wade to the patio chair,
-slumbering until night grows quiet.

Rising Sun

The dampness slipping along my forehead,
I place myself against the pillowed arch
of her thighs, pale to the softest light.

A flickering lamp taps across the hardwood floor.
I speak to her with the rise of the sun.

Vanish

The fullness of her hair swept as a tapestry,
smooth across her back.

I sank with the brim of my burning face-
surfacing flowered scents. The depth
of the orchid sang through her.

Her hands gripped the flesh of her thigh-
I listened to the bluebird, dripping in nights preludes.

From the spread of her lawn and the trim
of her garden, I poured in flashes.

Roaming the warm butters of a Winter's night
the raindrops of the morning hour
slid by the bedroom window. She dissolved into the fog
of night.

From Every Stitch

Her powdered skin swam across me.
I dipped through to the moist silks of her hair.

From hem and stitch, I fell upon her in patterns.

Each garment lay as a treasure.

Flickering and alive, I twined her as meadows
which tossed both pollens and seeds.

Pasture

Her shoulders enticed the hands which wrapped.
She grazed into the chest, endless fields of wheat.

Lips swelled against a pasture where
songs of the soon found river floods the edge of the bank.

The distant hills spread to the evergreen,
alive in clouds which sank.

Along the tired garden, she spoke of each throbbing rainfall.
She dissipated into nights blindness.

Looking upon Twilight

The rain slapped fluids on the narrow path.
I sit, feet propped and gather every scent of spice,
growing on the wandering trail.

I can touch you from a distance.
Droplets swoon to grass and flickering plant.

I see you upon the hyacinth
greedy and ready with purples.

Leaves melted on slight from warmth.
I watch as you sneer and slyly smile.
I grow damp and wet as you quiver in the twilight.

I reach my body, torn by the wind, which enters the home.
You display yourself in silver dust.

Observing the Shadow

Slouched on the patio chair, I rested as air sank,
fumbling through the tender grotto.

Feeling the penetration of the gold sun, crawling
behind cloudy pastures, I grazed my fingers through yours.

I looked upon the slowest of shadows
which thickened across us.

The cool of the forgiving sun and clouds
swallowed their way upon us. I watched her in rivets.

On towel she lay, perfumed from abdomen to breasts,
thighs to crossing legs.

In a quick moment, the sun returned. Roaming,
the breads of her, I puckered to the prowling heat.

From Woods Alone

Scattered growth, weeds and plants of an ancient mulch
lay sullen by jousting trees.

So gently, I rest the back of my neck;
I swim my thoughts through the generous pines

as I absorb their juices
stuck to my temples and chest.

A heavy shadow sulks across me in dancing prisms,
crafted by Spring.

Yesterday, the rains poured without ceasing.
I cling to the leaves which tug and unleash,

observing the blackened clouds which court the foliage
and drench the earth.

~

I walked into the fabric and threads of night
where the chill of my breathing saunters forth.

The waltz of the wind soothes across me.
I stop to look and notice the pouring creek.
Eager, I lay and rest.

Gathering in the Edge of the Woods

Swift, the wind tugged.
Trellising the grooming splash, a heavy breath-
fresh across her summit
I roam along soft doughy breasts.

I touched sweet perfumes of her linens, blouses and silky hair
which lay in blacks upon her shoulders.

By puddling pools of the creek
which gathered in the edge of the woods,
I held the cool smallness of her fragile hands.

By the crest of morning,
I left as she left and I listened to the purring stroke
of heavy breathing, a dancing mist.

Fallen Youth

The child tumbled across the grass hill,
settling in a spartic stretch of clay earth and creek.

Watching, I tangled through my pockets
lit a crumbling smoke.

Leisurely, the gloating sun pampered,
tucked behind a tense thinning cloud.

Evening, I wept to the purple sky
which trembled along the rims of the horizon
in patterns of red.

From Home to the Unburdening Bay

Here the birds nest, swoon upon the salted winds.

Boats slide through the fabrics of night,
tossing the moans of a sultry fog horn
which burroughs through the darkness implied.

In a blitz, the waters tug upon the rocky layered shore.

I hear her undress to the nooks of his thumb and fingers.
Patiently, she giggles to the gulping bay
As the salt thickens to the tremoring breeze.

Last year, the sod and peet whisper to the carrying
rhythms of my flickering lawn. I can hear the leaves laugh
upon the robes of threading clouds.

Seasons by the Bay

Her eyes, warm as cascading sheets of water
caressing the shoreline, tangled into me.

The clams relishing into the press of the sand;
I held her mouth against mine, then fell upon her.

~

Into the Winter flakes, powdering the chapped white
caps upon the water, I stood and recalled your touch.

By Spring, the water warmed and I wade
into the crests and scurry of the bay and cove.

Summer, the prowl of the rising sun, always rising;
hot flesh against crisp splashing foams.

~

Autumn and your leaves and drifting petals
sulk across my shoulders as I tremble to your lips.

As the Sky Spreads

Warm, buttery yellows spread into the pull of the sky.
Walking through this stretch of road,
I paused and pat the moist cloth along my forehead.

Yesterday, the grooming clouds shadowed across me.
Now, I blister in the mad heat
-thinking of you.

Guidance

The Summer grasses wilted with the scalding sun.
Later that year, you told me you heard them cry.

When the rain moistened the meadows and fields,
I heard you laugh.

Against the seeds of the earth, I walked
into the endless forests and passed the reaching trees.

~

You followed me past the pine needles and cones,
warning me of the approaching Autumn
which leads to Winter.

Parting

I lay by the nakedness of your full, pale breasts.
Peering through the bedroom window,
The clouds fill the tender sky.

I reach to you as you touch my hand.
The lawn, alive in greens, holds each dew drop
Along the reaching blade.

We watch as the sun fades.

~

Days pass.

I think of you.

Morning Alone

I settled across the dusty bed,
soaked in drifts of linens
and perfumes which linger as the low lying
clouds, soothing the brim and stretching
eaves of my home.

Finding smooth passage to her,
I sulked into the crawl of the dreams
which loosened her clothes;

by midday, the clouds had lifted
and each scent of Spring
molded to the edges of my face, torso, and wrapping arms.

The Willow Tree

The length of your bloomed, full hair
hung as a tapestry; the willow
bowed in hushing reverence to the pour
of a soft breeze.

From the silent gestures of your
glistening soft skin, I turned
to my bay window which stretched across
the distant flickering sun.

The buds along the gentle willow tree
perched and quivered with the roaming
branches. I remained quiet until the break of day.

Spreading Lips by Moonlight

Thinking of you, I could taste
the sweet paints of your smooth spreading lips.

Humid moisture danced across me
as I reached the breeze which danced
Through in mumbling voices

of breath; the light of this soft moon
fluttered through the tree leaves
which neighbored twig and branch

of the meadow where you lay.

I watched the slumbering log and lay still, silent.
The touch of your soothing mouth
moistened as the dew drops of nightfall.

The flashing winds spread through our hair
and groomed through until our burning faces
opened to daylight.

Orchid

Beyond the warm light of the sun,
I removed an orchid from the soft pampering
earth. Placing a petal on the edge of my tongue,

your sweet flavor drove through
to hot oils burning through my fingers and throbbing chest.

Wandering thoughts of you, the breeze flourished
against my face. Days later, I glistening in the garden pond

could see your image.

I walked the grassy trail, searching for the quiet
tender moist fields where I left you ages ago.

Throwing Rocks

The stream plowed through the creviced earth.

I sat, so close, watching the slight rippling water
ease the rocks which sank into the muds.

Kelp clung in wavering promises of glinted
shadows, nearing slight dashes of the moon.

The fern reached to the grassy bed.
Each flutter of wind frolicked through;

I heard her laugh to greens which touched
her naked feet. Placing her on the base of my

postured legs, we sat silent counting the rocks
which sank through to the channel, giving slight
ripples along the filmy surface.

Oak

The great oak invited a swift, cool breeze
from the damp sky at twilight.

Standing close, I gathered a few acorns,
placed them in my deep pockets

and went roaming the otherwise empty field.

Soft Thoughts

I thread my fingers through the bloomed,
full silks of your chestnut hair.

I whisper to you in eager fugues
as you loosen your blouse and crawl upon my
torso and quivering face.

In the most early of hours, I watch
the candle spill warm wax.

The wind rattles the walls of this ancient home
where thoughts proclaim.

Forested Hills

I settled upon the valley with eyes,
gleaming to the vast forested hills.

Early Spring buds quiver to the breeze,
spreading barks in splintering fibers.

In a hush, the branches danced.
I heard the lusty earth moan in melting
mulches where I rest, tired
from an endless hike.

From the resting slope of the boasting summit,
the ground stood, nearer to frozen, offering
a frosted gift to boots and passing denim.

The mountain creek slapped in rhythms
as I washed the cool sweat from my face.

Feeling the touch of you along
my nape and heavy shoulders,
I softened to the crest which glistens with the prowling sun.

Loosening Blouse

Low clouds dreamt through the fields,
which soon fell to the crowds,
the thick evergreen woods.

Upon reaching the first full, damp spruce,
I stopped and looked upon the glance
of your trembling eyes, coated in glaze.

I touched the soft paleness of your fragile hand
and softly quivered to the loosened
buttons along your slipping blouse.

Walking home, I stopped by the drip of the moist
trembling grass.

I felt the graze of your loose hands
as the fields grew tender with a fullness
From each towering tree.
I smiled and stepped into the brush and thicket of you.

Osprey

The river fed the smooth silks of the bay.
Tired waves greeted in foamed white caps
as frosted breath spread across the shore.

I cast my way to channel
which sank in soot and dancing kelp.

Then, in a quiet moment, I watched the osprey
thread the way across the gauze of the thin morning air.

The Pear Tree

Dedicate to: Nash and Darla Guide

Broad and roaming, the pear tree sank
into the grooming scents of minerals.
Soft, inviting soil suckled upon the tangled roots.

~

He stood and for a brief moment-
feeling the flesh which spread
along both lips and tongue.

Tenderly, she smiled and snapped the skin.

He warmed in butters and oils as she patiently
touched his neck and draped a hand of fingers
through his full wrestling hair.

Soils and Blackbirds

I placed the berry between my teeth, then snapped.
Juices dripped from lip to tongue.

In a moment, I stood still and heard the blackbird sing.

I gathered verbs of the fertile earth.
Quietly, I went my way. The grasses lay as a carpet
while finding home, resting bricks upon the inviting soil.

Standing by the Fence

Upon western winds, I roam searching
silence, the glancing sky, which feathers in inks.

I taste the hour of midnight as clouds fall
and find their way against stone and grass.

Into the wrapping arms of her,
I stand against the stretch of the pale picket fence.

This wind has no forgiveness as it slaps
against the sulking fields and presses

-tight through each strand of my heavy brown hair.

Diamond

Dew drops glimmer as the face of the diamond.
I moistened in tremors along mornings breath
which held my shaking body, loosened in shards.

The throbbing winds shook the house.
I gripped silently the dance of the grass fields
which spread along in greens.
In the earliest hour, I looked through
the old greasy window.

I smiled to the flood; mud rose in soft penetration.

Star Gazing

I walk through late Winter gales.
Near the ocean, I feel salts groom my face and stringy hair.

By nightfall, the clouds thin and spread
the shoreline like gauze.

Shuffled Leaves

Spring wind visits the rich forest.
I stop by the elm tree and rest.

I smell the spices of heavy mulch.
Looking up, leaves loosen and by evening.
I leave this place with puzzles dancing on the ground.

Camp

The forest vines coil along branches
as I perch on a long stretch of stone.

Fires flicker into the dry trees
while wood crackles and snaps.

By morning, the earth dampens
as smoke fills the air.

Idle Passages

Tucked beneath the pines,
I watch the sloping hills and their dancing branches.

Across me, a musty scent drifts
-filling the air.

Morning approaches and I step on the rocky path.

By noontime, I lose my way.

Fog's Arrival

Foam spreads along the water, gushing
across the endless lake.

My eyes soften to the faint traces of evening's light.

Washing my face and hands, white clouds suSlumber

The clouds pull as thread of an old garment.

I watch the hills comb the mist as soft wind
broods through the trees fingers.

Now nightfall, I drift into the feathers of my pillow,
pale white.

Clarity Waits

The storm swept the valley which sulked
-mumbling ferns.

Looking in sorrow to the hillside,
each leaf of each tree smoothed with raindrops.

Soon, the heavy ash clouds will lift
-I will sleep by the willow tree,
sheltered in quivering branches.

Elder Trees

Moist by the riverbank, hyacinths
sweeten the air.

Clouds lift and I look to the pasture,
spreading onion stalks and deep green
mint leaves.

Following the slender trail, I dissolve into the woodlands.
It moans my name from root to trembling treetop.

Watching Crows

Soft, pensive rain pats upon my garden.
Spring flowers entice.

This staff, snug in my grip, spends a moment
thick in the mud beneath me.

With moments ahead, I hike through the forest.
I hear the crows take flight with a cool breeze.

Fields Tucked between Mountains

Here, sleeping, the showers bloom through nearby fields.

Hearing a scattered slap of mountain winds,
I soothe to them and smile upon each rocky face.

When I awaken in the damp morning light,
raindrops nurse each grass blade and glimmer
to the lilac bush.

Thin Lips

Softly perched on a blossoming twig,
the goldfinch glistens jade green buds.

Quietly, I kiss her on the paints of her thin roaming lips.

After a moment, I look to the crest of the sky, filled
with cottony clouds.

Finches dart to the reaching treetops.

Afternoon Moisture

I walk the garden in search of bounty and harvest.
Now afternoon, I taste the richness of the earth.

Close to you by the burning fire, I drift
across your powdered skin.

As we touch, the garden grass upholds
each trembling raindrop.

Passage

I sulk into the bones of the earth,
riddled in clays.

The creek pulls, wedging the soft pulps of this bed of marrow.

I hear your voice
as it rattled through the pine trees.

Robe

I look at her, frail beneath the moon.
Shadows cling to her as a robe.

When I touch her cool face,
I feel the silks of nightfall.

Together, we walk through the moist meadow.
Close, our hands twine like ribbons.

Soft

White and green leaves cover the ground
and shake along the forest floor.

You loosen your shoes by the bedroom hearth.

I touch your breath with this gentle wind
scouring through each woodland maze.

As the Trees Echo

The maple leaves wave through the
sleeves of a crisp, cool wind.

As the jades of the spreading branches tremble,
I think of your flickering hair, tossing sweet scents.

By midday, I kiss the gems of your lips.

Veils

Wintertime, white veils of satin blown snow blindly.

Watching you undress, I fell quiet
with the approach of Spring,
all it's warmth and nakedness.

From thicket to fields of swaying barley,
I remember the softness of your skin.

Acorn

Winds broom the shaking buds which
house by the slap of the river.

By water's bank, the driftwood spools
in iced white foamy caps.

I can hear the leaves speak of last harvest.

I walk the edge of each spindling creek.

Greens open as acorns begin their cushioned descent.

Mountains and Forests

With a heavy glaze of snow, cliffs paused with endless rocks,
boast of their mountain face.

When Winter blinks, I awaken to witness the flicker
of blooming plants.

I close my tender eyes and watch
you walk these combing wooded trails.

Resting beneath the spruce, each slender needle
slices the wind of late March.

Cove

Reaching. I slip my palms to the fullness
of your cotton pouches and I roam for the seeds
which bury through each wave of flickering foam.

She tells me there drifts an ocean inside of her.

With the shatter of morning light, I almost hear
the lull of each soaring seagull which quivers to the edge
of my ears and your eyes which dance as a lighthouse
-looking upon me.

So by the end of morning and the past soft sand of night,
I bring you the reeds of my touch and pause
at the glance of full, wet buoys.

I cascade across your gentle heavy breasts;
quietly, we watch the peach skies of morning fade
across the tender slant of beach and kelp ridden cove.

Eastern Trail

I look upon the leaves, curled edges which fall to dust.

The sky fattens like smoke as the winds scurry through,

each sulking gown of the forests trees as they moan

in the rhythms of dancing branches,
soon to fall upon the earth.

~

I hear the sky moan. I pause for a moment, then briskly

walk away as the tamp of my boot still knows it's way home.

~

As I near the eastern trail, I will always
see the sun pierce the horizon.

        Thin clouds, broad mountains,
        be patient -soon they will shine as hills.

About the Author

Donny Barilla, a poet covering the realms: human intimacy, nature, mythology, theology, and man's relationship with death and the departed, has been writing for over three decades. He writes daily and strives to renew himself as an artist from page to page and body of work to body of work. Very seldom does he take a break from writing as he views it as a full-time job. He lives a reclusive lifestyle and finds himself clinging close to nature and all her elements. His home state of Pennsylvania strikes chords of poetic depth about him as he finds loveliness from cornfield to meadow. Whether it's feelings of love, intimacy, or a special closeness, he maintains the feeling that death does not take these with him/her to the grave. Emotions and feeling outlast the flesh of the human body. Human intimacy draws near an enigmatic spiritual passion which conquers all on the prismatic scale of experience. When speaking of mythology Donny says, "myths were created to make sense of feelings which are complicated by very nature. They are perhaps more easily understood through persons greater than oneself. As for theology, a disciplined aspect, incorporates quite finely with passions and secured poetic comforts.

https://twitter.com/BarillaDonny

www.ingramcontent.com/pod-product-compliance
Lightning Source LLC
Chambersburg PA
CBHW032227080426
42735CB00008B/744